G

is for

Goal
Magick

Kitchen Table Magick Series

by
G. Alan Joel

Esoteric School of Shamanism & Magic

Contact Information: alan@shamanschool.com
Visit my website: www.shamanschool.com

Publisher: Esoteric School of Shamanism and Magic, Inc.

Disclaimer and Legal Notice:
The Esoteric School of Shamanism and Magic has made every effort to ensure,
at the time of this writing, that the information contained in this book is as
accurate as possible. The publisher and author make no warranties or
representation with respect to the completeness, fitness, accuracy, applicability,
or appropriateness of this book's contents. This book's information is provided
strictly for entertainment and educational purposes. Should you choose to use
or apply the ideas provided in this book, you take full responsibility for your
own actions. The publisher and author provide no guarantee that your life will
improve in any way should you choose to use the information presented in this
book. The ability of the information provided in this book to provide self-help
and life improvement to the reader is entirely dependent upon the reader. The
reader's ability to gain positive results from the information presented in this
book is entirely dependent on the amount of time the reader devotes to the
application of the material in this book, the willingness of the reader to dedicate
time and effort to learning the materials presented in this book, as well as the
reader's own belief system, which may help or hinder the reader's ability to
benefit from this book's materials. Since each reader differs according to
willingness and openness to the information available in this book, the author
and publisher cannot guarantee success or improvement for every individual
reader. Neither the publisher nor the author assumes responsibility for the
reader's actions, or whether the information is used for negative or positive
purposes. The information contained in this book is drawn from tribal
traditions—both modern and ancient—as well as the author's 30 plus years of
experience researching and teaching this material to students. The information
in this book is presented as interpreted by the author, and, as such, may or may

not be entirely accurate. In no way should the information presented in this book be a substitute for advice from health or mental health professionals. The author and publisher are not liable—or in any way responsible—for actions that the reader may or may not take as a result of reading the information contained in this book. The reader assumes full responsibility for his or her own actions and choices with regard to how he or she chooses to use the information in this book. The reader is strongly encouraged to choose to use the information provided in this book responsibly.

Goal Magick Blessing

Child of Wonder, Child of Flame
Nourish My Spirit and Protect My Aim.
Guardians of goals, supporters of aim
Hear my call, as I invoke my claim.
As a planetary citizen I have a right
To manifest my wishes, dreams burning bright.

New Year's Resolutions have failed me prior
So I seek now goal magick as the path to the higher.
Support now my aims before me today
Guide me on my path as I walk, without delay.

Getting in my own way happens I know
Show me how I get in my way, cause my goals to slow.
Magickal elemental forces create my magickal self
Highlight my strengths, so the best parts be the essence of
myself.

With the help of energies of Sun, Sky, and Earth
Magick will show me my magickal self's true worth.
A price I have to pay, of this I am aware and sure
Willing am I to pay my chosen price, so my path stays clear.

Thus my will, so mote it be!

Free Gift Offer

To thank you for purchasing this book, I'd like to give you a

100% FREE GIFT

Learn more about your free magickal gift.

Click Here to Access Your Free Gift

Find a complete list of magickal resources on _G. Alan Joel's Author Page_. These resources are constantly updated so check back often!

Table of Contents

Introduction to Kitchen Table Goal Magick

"The world is full of magic things, patiently waiting for our senses to grow sharper."
~ W. B. Yeats

A Note About This Introduction

This book is one of a series of books in the Kitchen Table Magick series. Each book in the series addresses a specific area of magick (love, money, psychic development, etc.), and is written in a simple "recipe" format for people who want to use magick in their lives immediately. The Kitchen Table Magick series is akin to a Julia Childs recipe book, only these books contain magickal recipes for people to cook up some miraculous and magickal manifestations in their lives.

Because this series was designed so that each person could pick and choose to read just the books that pertain to their current life situation, each book is meant to be readable as a stand alone book. To introduce the new reader to the series, this introduction to the series is repeated at the beginning of each book. If you have already read one or more books in this series, please feel free to jump ahead to the recipes that interest you. At the same time, some people feel that reviewing the introduction, as well as the "Rules and Tips," is helpful before diving in. In magickal circles, your will is the guideline so choose whichever route best suits you... the Universe and magickal beings will follow!

What is Magick?

Many people have multiple different ideas about what magick is or can be. For the sake of clarity, here is what we know about magick after more than 35 years of study and practice. Magick is a precision science! It is also:

- The science of deliberate creation.
- The science of effective prayer.
- The science of manifesting Higher Will (substitute whatever Higher Force is most familiar to you) on the energetic and material planes.
- The science of heightened awareness, selective perception, and dynamic, harmonious relationships.
- The study of intention (as per Aleister Crowley, one of the greatest magickal practitioners in history).
- The system of creation, not coercion. Note: The word manipulation is often used in conjunction with magick, but manipulation simply means the use of the hands. It should be an "OK" word without a lot of charge, but currently it is used mostly to mean coercion. Look it up!
- The principle that every intentional act is a magickal act! Magick gives us the ability to communicate with beings on all levels, and allows us to understand, through direct experience, the actual workings of the Universe.
- The traditional path of spiritual growth.
- Not extraordinary knowledge. It is the "normal" way of life. We've just lost access to it. When you have this kind of knowledge in your understanding, you have the ability to resolve spiritual questions that otherwise become catechism. From a magickal point of view, catechism is not acceptable, since a practitioner must experience and verify everything for him or herself. It avoids the trap of dogma. In

past times, having a magickal foundation was essential so that we could talk directly to higher beings in the Universal hierarchy.

- Necessary to effective religious practice.
- The basis for all true sciences, based on personal observation. True science has nothing to do with the Western need for "proof," which introduces doubt into the equation.

There is some confusion as to how to spell the word "magick." There are three different commonly used spellings: magick, magic, and majick. Eliphas Levi first used the form "magick" to differentiate religious or ceremonial from stage magick. All forms of spelling are acceptable in what this author teaches.

"I've been studying mystical pursuits for over three decades now, and I've never had as much fun as I am with the Kitchen Table Magick series. Even though I have a lot of magickal knowledge, having fun with magickal rituals that are always fun is the perfect combination for me!"
~ John Silverman, Boise, ID

Is Magick Real?

Yes. Magick is very real and has existed as a precise science for thousands of years. Whether you use the word magick or another name, this spiritual practice is very real. Every single person can learn to do magick. We are ALL born with the talents and abilities that empower us to do magick. The only reason that magick seems so, well, magickal is that this society no longer teaches the art and science of magick. In the distant past, magickal study was just as important as math, science, or the arts. In fact, magick was and still is the birthright of EVERY planetary citizen.

Can you learn to do the kind of magick portrayed in the movies? Yes... and no. The movies are great at giving you a taste of what you can do with magick, but they are not very accurate. In the Harry Potter movies, for instance, the characters use their Wands for every magickal operation. In reality, you can only use the Wand to handle Air energies. Your Wand would actually explode or catch fire if you tried to use it to throw Firebolts and Fireballs as the characters do in the movie.

So what can you actually do with magick? Quite a lot. Here is a short list to get you started:

- Balance your energies for healing and manifestation
- Change old beliefs
- Defend yourself against physical and psychic attack
- Heal yourself and others
- Find hidden information and see possible futures (and change the future if you do not like the probable futures you divine)
- Psychically communicate with other beings
- Create sacred space
- Find lost people and objects
- Manifest what you want and need in life

At the very basis of magick is the understanding of the four elements: Air, Fire, Water, and Earth. Called elemental magick, these foundational elements are real. Air, Fire, Water and Earth are part of our natural everyday environment. What makes them magickal is the understanding of how they operate not just on the physical level, but also at the levels of Mind and Spirit.

For instance, while on the physical level Air is just the stuff we breathe, on the magickal levels Air is the conduit of psychic communication, enlightenment, understanding, dreaming, and more. If you want more of any of these things in your life, then you need more magickal Air. How do you get more magickal Air? Wear more Air colors, including white for communication and sky blue for enlightenment and understanding. To take this one step further, you could also use various magickal techniques to take on more Air to make your body lighter. Take on enough Air and you'll be able to levitate.

By just extending your understanding and use of the basic ingredients of nature, you are doing magick! Seen in this light, magick isn't all smoke and mirrors, nor is it the result of Hollywood special effects. Magick is the result of truly understanding and working with the very elements that are all around you.

One final note: Many masters, including Wayne Dyer, have said, "You'll see it when you believe it." The same is true for magick. In other words, the suspension of disbelief and the willingness not to exercise contempt prior to investigation are requirements for magick to be "real." Magick is all around us, and always is, but our ability to perceive and use the forces of magick depends on our willingness to be open. No one else can show it to you, only your direct experience and observation can "prove" or demonstrate to you that magick is real.

Kitchen Table Goal Magick at Work...

We receive all kinds of stories and testimonials from happy successful students. Read the example below to discover how Goal Magick works in real life...

Goal Magick Helps the Clueless

Since I can remember I have known exactly what I wanted, and how to get what I wanted. Imagine my surprise when I found myself clueless and bewildered standing at a crossroads, knowing which direction I wanted to go, yet having no clue how to get there. The crossroads in my life offered me two options: either continue to vigorously pursue my career in internet marketing or change course completely and become a healer. Having suffered through multiple debilitating injuries during the past six years, the path of healing pulled at me like a magnet. I was attracted to the path of healing, but I had no idea what to do or how to move forward on that path.

So I turned to goal magick. I had been reading about goal magick on the blog of the Esoteric School of Shamanism and Magic, and liked the fact that goal magick didn't require me to know how I would achieve my goal, just that I needed to state my goal clearly. Magick would do the rest. For someone feeling as lost and confused as I was at that point in my life, goal magick felt like a lifeline.

The Goal: The Healing Path

The only goal I had was to follow the healing path. I did not feel any pull to continue with internet marketing, even though I was able to generate a steady income from that work. Having experienced some powerful healing of my own disastrous injuries during the past six years, I felt that I wanted to pay that knowledge forward, somehow. Since I had nothing but the desire to walk the healing path, I wrote my goal that simply. I asked the powers and guardians of goal magick to help me walk my healing path, showing me the way, guiding my actions and thoughts, and bringing the right people and events into my life. Armed with the knowledge that magick could and would answer my call if I but asked with gratitude and listened with care, I turned my attention to my part of the path: dealing with my own resistance.

Removing Resistance

The powers and beings of goal magick would, I knew, help me if I but asked. I had felt this many times when I needed healing for my own injuries. But reading more about goal magick, I also learned that I had to do my part to walk this new journey of healing. What was my part? To remove the resistance caused by my magickal personality type. Each person on Earth has a dominant magickal elemental personality, and some people also have a secondary elemental type. In reading about the elemental types on the Esoteric School website, I discovered that the Air element was dominant in my elemental personality. I also discovered that Fire was a secondary elemental part of my magickal personality. I read through the elemental types on the Esoteric School website and found that their abbreviated descriptions of each element were very helpful. Since I was a dominant Air and secondary Fire type, I carefully copied down the descriptions below so that I could refer to them whenever I needed to refresh my memory:

Air
Seeing, breathing, speaking, hearing, planning, thinking, believing, memorizing, communicating, learning, teaching, information, ideas, wisdom, understanding, worry, sensation, awareness, opinions, data, memory, mind.

Fire
Energy, power, will, desire, anger, pain, motivation, radiance, passion, initiative, aggression, limitation, endeavors, activity, creative, willingness, urge, inspiration, excitability, courage, bravado, compulsion, fanaticism, frustration, resentment, rage, freedom.

I could definitely see Air as the dominant element of my magickal personality. I have always been a talker, worrier, planner, gatherer of information, person of strong opinions, and possessed of a relentless memory bank. Driving all of those aspects of personality, my secondary element, Fire, meant I also had energy to burn, motivation that pushed through any barriers, creativity that wouldn't quit, and subject to rage, anger, and pain. Being full of bravado, I often participated in activities that required a great deal of courage... and were often quite dangerous. Hence, I had a lot of pain in my life at all levels.

After meditating on these magickal elements of my personality, I focused on talking, worrying, anger, will, and pain as characteristics that caused the most resistance in my life. As I used the Walking Litany of the Navajo Beauty Way to communicate with the Universe, I received messages that confirmed my "take" on the elemental aspects that caused the greatest resistance in my life. The other message I received was that my continuous output of Air and Fire into my life caused a great deal of trouble. I had never thought of my life this way, but after receiving this message I could definitely see how my strong will, my tendency to be quick to anger, and my ever worrying mind caused me to say and do things that got me in all kinds of troublesome situations. I saw how these "expressions" of Air and Fire created all kinds of extra work for me in my life.

My Chosen Price: Silence

What could I do to reduce the resistance caused by my constant output of Air and Fire into my life? Good question. Luckily the information on goal magick suggested choosing a "price to pay" to reduce resistance of this kind. At first I didn't understand what kind of price I might pay to reduce the resistance caused by my elemental make-up. But then I realized that the word "output" was key in this. I constantly outputted thoughts, words, opinions, expressions of worry, anger, pain-driven rage, and a powerful will that tended to run other people over as a matter of course.

I meditated on this problem for several days, and finally decided that the best price I could pay into the success of walking my path was silence. The old adage says "Silence is golden." In my case, I realized that if I could stop talking about my pain, anger, will, opinions, and worries, my silence might be even more valuable than "golden"... the results of my silence might be priceless.

So, with a deep breath, I decided to hold my tongue as much as I could. I decided to communicate only when necessary, and to otherwise hold silence as my daily price to pay into my goal of walking my healing path. I suspected that the powers and beings were laughing a little, since they had probably been giving me the guidance and answers I sought all along, only I couldn't hear them because I was constantly talking and expressing rather than listening. When I felt worried, angry, the need to enforce my will, or the need to lash out because of my accumulated pain, I decided that I would endeavor to keep my silence, no matter what was going on around me or inside me.

I had no doubt that the price of silence was very high for an Air/Fire personality type, but at the same time I realized it was the only logical price to pay. I knew there would be days and times when I would fail to pay this price, but I could do nothing but endeavor to persevere.

The Journey Along My Healing Path

As I had guessed, the price of silence was a difficult one to achieve day to day, moment to moment. But I did the best I could and the results were spectacular. When I was able to be quiet and silent for the most part, I received all kinds of guidance and help from the powers and guardians of goal magick. I received information about what to do and how to do it. I got regular downloads from those powers and beings about how to proceed on my path... when I was able to achieve silence. When I could be quiet both inside and outside, I found that I gained even more information. The Sun Candle ritual with Directors and Limiters was so powerful that I couldn't wait to light my Sun Candle daily. And the Walking Litany added similar amounts of guidance and information.

My healing path looks nothing like I expected. Of course, I knew very little about what to expect, but this path has been filled with surprises. For the most part, my life looks a lot like it always has on the outside. I still work on the internet when I am guided to do so. Other times I run into beings who need my healing help, and I am guided as to how best to offer healing energy. Other times beings coming into my energetic Healing Circle, which I created based on directions offered by the goal magick angels and guides. In the Healing Circle, I don't need to do anything but hold the circle open... what I call "holding the space." Beings seem to be able to come into the circle at will, find the tools they need to heal, and apply those tools without help from me. The Healing Circle is totally invisible except to beings (in body and in Spirit form) who seek the energy it offers. And since I don't speak of it to anyone because of my price of silence, no one else knows about it.

Silence has been a journey in and of itself. It has allowed me to let go of so many things on so many levels. Silence means that I can no longer verbally attack others, or speak my will that forces others to do as I demand or risk my wrath. Silence has taught me that if I leave many bothersome situations alone, they simply heal or fix themselves without my help. In this way, my healing path is about leaving things be, knowing that my interference is often more of a hindrance than help. Silence has become a touchstone of my healing path, and I could not be more surprised. Silence is indeed most golden, and I am loving walking this path, even the parts of the path that seem to run straight uphill. Those are the times when I find it most difficult to hold my tongue, but I am getting better. As I learn to make silence the first and last thought, I walk the healing path with greater and greater ease. I cannot be more pleased with my adventure with goal magick! Even with nothing but a bare bones idea of the path, I have been able to make my way with the help of the guardians of goal magick. I am most grateful.

~ Helen Greer, Galesburg, IL

What is Kitchen Table Magick?

(Note: this information is in all books in the Kitchen Table Magick series. If you have already read this information, feel free to move on to the Ingredients of Kitchen Table Goal Magick... Enjoy!)

Kitchen Table Magick is exactly what it sounds like—a series of simple recipes that you can literally "cook up" at your kitchen table using household ingredients from your own pantry and cupboard.

The Kitchen Table Magick books have been created for ordinary people who want to mix up a little magick in their lives without all the fancy rituals, but simply with everyday ingredients that can be found in the kitchen pantry, bathroom medicine cabinet, or even stuffed in the back of the junk drawer.

The goal of these books is to allow anyone with the desire to learn this craft to mix up magick literally at the kitchen table using simple recipes. What goes into a simple recipe?

- Everyday items as ingredients
- Easy to follow instructions that don't require years of training
- Procedures that take less than two hours from start to finish
- Built-in expertise that allows the magick to do the heavy lifting
- Some friendly advice on how you can help your magickal recipe provide the best results

- Oh, and a few little rules and guidelines about magickal practice in this specific arena that will keep you safe and sound, magickally speaking, when you use these recipes

Kitchen Table Magick Equals:
Quick – Effective – Safe – Everyday Use – Ordinary Affordable Ingredients

Why Use Kitchen Table Magic?
- Everyone can do magick
- Magick should be simple, effective, and start working right away, else it is not magick
- Not everyone has the time or resources to enroll in a school
- People ask us for magickal help in hundreds of emails everyday... Kitchen Table Magick is designed to help these very people.
- Of the many areas of life, most people only seem to need help in one or two areas, so you need only buy those Kitchen Table Magick books that apply to your needs
- Magick is for the masses, and should be accessible, affordable, and simple to do. This is what our teacher taught us, and this is the legacy we are paying forward as well
- While there are many more advanced forms of magick, these books are an introduction to that world so that you can dabble, experiment, try things out, see the result, adjust and amend, and generally have fun... just as you would cooking a meal in your kitchen.
- This book is not for the major foodie, but is perfect for the person who needs magickal help right here, right now!

Who Should Use These Recipes?

- You and anyone you know who would like a little more magick and a little less ordinary reality in their lives.
- Anyone who needs help RIGHT now and doesn't have time to fly to India or Sedona to sit at the feet of a guru.
- Anyone who does not have access to anything but a computer for help and guidance.
- Anyone who wants to do magick and then forget it (all while quietly watching the magick "do its thing").
- Anyone who wants affordable, down to earth magick they can do with regular ingredients in the comfort of home.

When to Use Kitchen Table Magic: Anytime...

- You need help.
- You don't want to do all the heavy lifting (leave that to the angels, Spirit guides, animal totems, and so forth).
- You seem stuck in a rut or corner with no way out.
- You've been struggling with a problem for a long time and need a resolution.
- You don't know what to do but you need to do SOMETHING.
- You'd like to learn how to practice the craft.
- You want to live a more magickal life and stop dealing with ordinary hassles all the time.

How Do We Know These Recipes Work?

- We teach a slew of these recipes in one-day workshops all over the country, via teleconference, and via video conference. We also email them to people as part of our school's service work, or post them on our blogs and articles library.
- We have used them for over 35 years and still do every single day – literally tested out at our own kitchen tables for over 35 years, and at thousands of kitchen tables around the world for a quarter century or more.

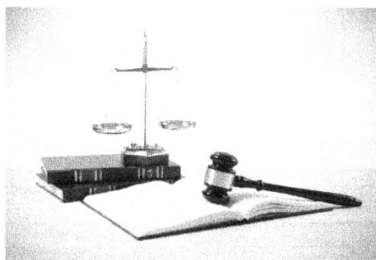

A Few Rules and Tips About Kitchen Table Magick

"In the practice of magic and shamanism, every practitioner needs to follow Universal Rules to practice these arts safely and effectively."
~ Joanna Drummond

As with any game, the game of life has its own set of rules. Specifically, the spiritual side of life has rules. Play by those rules and you will stay safe and easily attract what you want into your life. Break those rules and all types of unwanted consequences happen.

These "spiritual rules" are ones that have been observed, both in personal spiritual practice and spiritual practice with various associated groups and teachers. These rules universally govern any spiritual practice, and appear to be in effect whether you know them or not. Unlike ethics and morals, which change with culture and time, these spiritual rules appear to have remained the same throughout time, unchanging, like physical and scientific rules.

The rules in the following section are adapted from *Rules of the Road*, as created by George Dew, co-founder of the Church of Seven Arrows. There are two major rules, which are common to most spiritual practices, along with some minor rules that are specific to our form of magickal practice.

Two Major Rules

These two rules will probably sound familiar, as they appear in most major religions and spiritual practices, most probably because they are common-sense and apply not just to spiritual practice, but to life as well.

First Rule: Golden Rule or Law of Karma

This first rule is literally a "golden oldie":

What you do to the environment or to other beings in the environment brings similar effects back to you in your life.

Often recognized as the Golden Rule or the Law of Karma, this rule tops the list because it reminds all spiritual practitioners of potential unwanted "rebound" or side effects. As your spiritual power, focus, and abilities grow, this rule will have an ever greater impact on your life unless you exercise caution. The Universe responds more strongly and powerfully to those with focus, power, and ability.

Note: As humanity moves further in the Aquarian Age, many spiritual practitioners have seen more effects from this rule occur faster. In the past, effects of this rule that often took lifetimes to manifest now occur in minutes, days, weeks, or months. In this particular time in Earth's history, karma seems to operate under a "pay as you go" system. Simply stated, expect the effects of the Law of Karma to occur quickly.

Second Rule: The Judgment of "Good and Bad" According to the Universe

This second rule adds clarity and detail to the first rule described previously:

If you are unsure whether your acts are "good or bad"-- that is, whether those acts are in keeping with universal laws on this planet—the Universe will reflect its judgment back to you quickly, according to the "pay as you go" Law of Karma.

This law holds as true for individuals as it does for entire communities, states, nations, or other organized groups. If you are still unsure of the feedback you receive from the Universe, check areas such as your level of health, the soundness of social relationships, your prosperity or lack of, sufficiency of various needs in life, and even your "luck" with appliances and machines. If your luck appears to be consistently poor, then you are probably acting contrary to universal governing laws, regardless of your intentions. The Universe cares about what you do more than what you intend.

Additional Detailed Rules

The following rules offer more detailed standards by which to measure your acts or the acts of others to determine whether these acts are in accordance with universal laws.

- Do nothing that will harm another being unless you are willing to suffer similar or greater harm. What the Universe considers "harm" may be different than what you consider harm.

- Do not bind another being unless you are willing to be similarly bound. An example of binding someone is doing acts in attempt to coerce a specific other person to love you. There is no problem with attracting your soul mate into your life, but doing acts that attempt to coerce a specific other person to love you is a type of binding.

- Never use your spiritual abilities in vain, to show off, or to boost your pride. Using your spiritual abilities from a place of pride usually causes the Universe to bring instant backlash into your life.

- If you choose to charge money or barter for using your spiritual abilities in the service of others, avoid charging extremely high prices. Charge prices for using methods comparable to other professionals, such as an attorney or accountant.

- Never use any spiritual word, chant, litany, or similar "device" unless you are confident in your understanding of its methods, intents, and effects.

- When undertaking a major spiritual operation—one that will require significant effort or attempts to create a major effect in the world—use divination to determine whether you can safely benefit from such an operation, and to discover the obstacles you must overcome. Divination methods such as pendulum readings, channeling, meditation, and question circles (to name a few) can reveal hidden factors of which you may be unaware.

- In any spiritual endeavor, take your time, think it through, and do it right!

Unlike many mundane laws, you may notice that these Universal rules are considerably simpler. At the same time, while practicing any kind of magick you will be subject to these rules regardless of whether you know them or remember them. Luckily, the two major rules are quite easy to remember!

The Ingredients of Goal Magick

"Same dreams, fresh starts. I dare you to believe in yourself. You deserve all things magic."
~ overlyexclusive

In our goal-driven society, most of us are aiming to achieve one or more goals at any point in time. For instance, an associate at a law firm most likely has a goal of becoming a partner in a firm. Or a high school student might have the goal of being accepted into a good college. For most modern people, reaching a goal isn't enough. Instead of feeling a deep sense of satisfaction for a long period of time after reaching a goal, most people immediately turn their attention to the next goal.

With this kind of mentality, life becomes more like mountain climbing than living. As the old adage goes, we become more like "human doings" than "human beings." Our incessant need to achieve ever greater goals means that we rarely get to enjoy our achievements. We are brainwashed regularly by slogans such as, "Don't rest on your laurels"!

It's likely, then, that if you are reading this book, you are one of those goal-oriented people who want a little extra "magickal edge" to help you reach your goals even faster. There is absolutely nothing wrong with achievement or goals. But goal magick may not be what you think. While goal magick will definitely help you reach your goals more effectively and efficiently, the path of goal magick is very different from the mundane path of working longer and harder than everyone around you. The ingredients of goal magick focus on different aspects of your life to achieve the same ends, better and faster.

Level of Being versus Level of Doing

In magick there is an important phrase that is very important to goal magick:

"The level of your Being determines the level of your life."

In the ordinary world, this might sound like any other mantra or affirmation. If you've studied spiritual paths to greater achievement, this might sound like something from movies like *The Secret*, in which you imagine yourself driving a brand new Corvette daily to "attract" that car into your life.

But working on the level of your Being can be quite different than simply imagining and holding the vibration of what you want. Goal magick focuses on methods for raising the level of your Being so that the things you want will come more easily into your life.

The equation is quite simple: when you increase the level of your whole Being, every aspect of your life is also raised to a higher level so that the "achievements" you seek over the next hill will appear automatically. Why? Because your higher level of Being causes you to reach the top of that next hill ("achievement") without actual "doing" on your part. Instead of putting in all the extra overtime hours needed to go from associate to partner in a law firm, when you raise your level of Being you will automatically land in that partnership without direct effort. This is not to say that you won't have to work extra hours, just that when you raise your level of Being you may work fewer hours or you may find working those extra hours (and balancing the work load with the rest of your life) easier and more enjoyable. How do you raise the level of your Being? By focusing on a small, yet key, part of your life that will change your entire energetic makeup. For instance, one of our students had difficulty "moving up the world" because she could never quite finish the work projects she started at her job. At first, this student was quite excited about any new project, and this excitement gave her the energy to tackle the project. But as the project moved forward, and the nitty-gritty details became too boring, she quickly lost momentum and began searching for something new to fire her excitement.

To help her stay the course on any given project, as part of her coursework in the Esoteric School of Shamanism and Magic, she was asked to choose a tiny area of her life that reflected this lack of completion, and focus on improving her performance in that tiny area only. Once she reflected on this, she realized that her husband constantly complained that she never closed jar lids completely, so the next person to pick up the jar by the lid was likely to drop the jar and spill the contents. In a very small way, this woman never "completed" the action of closing jar lids by screwing them all the way shut. Thus her yearly magickal aim became to always be conscious of the jars she handled, and work on screwing the lids on completely. While this may sound like a silly exercise with no bearing on her job, she discovered that there was a direct correlation between her ability to screw jar lids all the way shut, and her ability to complete projects at work.

This exercise was effective because it raised the level of her Being in a specific area, so that the level of her performance in all areas of her life also improved. This exercise, though simple, increased the level of her Being by forcing her to be conscious for a few moments each day. Every second of increased consciousness increased her level of Being. With a greater level of Being, she then found herself more conscious and able to complete projects at work.

Your Magickal Being

While you may have a good idea of who you are in everyday life, another important aspect of goal magick is to look at who you are in terms of the Four Elements of Magick: Air, Fire, Water, and Earth. Most of us have a dominant magickal Element, and most of us also have a secondary magickal Element. Our Elemental makeup determines how we operate as magickal beings in life. For goal magick, each element has its helpful characteristics, as well as characteristics that cause resistance in reaching our goals in life. Knowing who you are as a magickal being, and working to reduce the effects of the resistant characteristic, can give you a big "leg up" in your goal magick. Here's a short list of the areas of our lives governed by each Element:

Air
Seeing, breathing, speaking, hearing, planning, thinking, believing, memorizing, communicating, learning, teaching, information, ideas, wisdom, understanding, worry, sensation, awareness, opinions, data, memory, mind

Fire
Energy, power, will, desire, anger, pain, motivation, radiance, passion, initiative, aggression, limitation, endeavor, activity, creative, willingness, urge, inspired, excitable, courage, bravado, compulsion, fanaticism, frustration, resentment, rage, freedom

Water
Emotions, feelings, intuition, compassion, empathy, sympathy, knowing, devotion, quest, aspiration, intention, appreciation, integrity, harmony, beauty, balance, serenity, fluidity, grief, apathy, joy, love

Earth
strength, money, foundation, endurance, structure, mundane world, serenity of beingness, solidity, boundaries, permanence, land, commerce, products, confidence, loyalty, persistence, stubbornness, fortress, security, anchor, barter, substance, body, base, possessions

In this book, we will give you the tools and skills to boost the strengths and soften the resistance associated with your Elemental makeup. Because you bring your Elemental makeup to bear in everything you think, feel, do, and be, maximizing the benefits and minimizing the resistance of your Elemental makeup will speed the results of your goal magick greatly.

Your Magickal Price

As in the everyday world, there is a price to be paid for every goal you achieve. Going back to the previous example of the goal of becoming a partner in your law firm, the everyday price you would pay is working long hours, doing as partners ask, being a team player, and so forth. The price you pay in reaching such a major goal is not difficult to define, but can be difficult to achieve because it requires great effort and can wreak havoc in other areas of your life (such as your family life).

Luckily, with goal magick you don't need to pay such a heavy price to achieve your goals. Instead of paying with long hours and an unbalanced life, a magickal price is something that you voluntarily choose to pay to increase your level of Being, and decrease the resistance to reaching your goals. Your magickal price is different from the everyday price you pay for the same goal. First, your magickal price is something that no one else may notice. Second, you get to name your magickal price rather than having it imposed on you from an outside source, such as the partners in the law firm.

Your chosen magickal price is something that you choose to give up or take on to change your Being in some fundamental way. For instance, if the level of your Being is being affected by your anger, you may choose to take on the "cortothalamic pause" as your price. The cortothamalic pause is a two-second pause you take before you express your anger. In these two seconds, you ask yourself, "Do I really need/want/choose to get angry now?" Or you might ask yourself, "What effects will my anger have on this situation, or on my goals?" This tiny little pause, the span of a breath, gives you the chance to pay a personal price that will increase your level of Being... and thus speed your movement toward your goals. Even if you take a cortothalamic pause, and still express your anger, your level of Being will increase. Any time you are focused and conscious of yourself and your situation, your level of Being increases. As the level of your Being increases, the level of your life will also increase.

Your magickal price need not be high or difficult. For instance, if you have difficulty changing habits, pay a small price that changes a tiny habit. One student chose to change the hand with which he used to open doors. Being right-handed, he typically used his right hand to open doors. For his magical price, he chose to use his left hand to open doors. Amazingly enough, by just paying this small price he found that he had far less resistance in reaching his goals. What's more, no one noticed that he changed the hand he used to open doors, but people did notice that his personality became more flexible and less rigid.

You don't need to be an over-achiever when it comes to choosing your magickal price. Just pick a price that is related to one or more aspects that are keeping you from raising your level of being. If you talk too much or are a poor listener, choose to listen fully when talking to another person on the phone. How? Just close your eyes as you talk on the phone, avoid multi-tasking, and wait until the other person has completed his or her comments before responding (i.e., don't cut off the other person just so you can get your comments in). See how simple your magickal price can be? The more fun your magickal price, the more likely you are to pay it. So pick a whimsical magickal price, practice it with joy, and have fun!

Goal Magick Recipes

Appetizers: Define the "What" and "Who" of Your Goals

Define Your Goals: Write, Light, and Be Bright

Discover Your Magickal Type: What's Your Magickal Personality?

"I've studied a lot of different methods to determine personality type, so I thought I knew a lot about my own personality. I was truly surprised when I discovered my magical personality. It 'filled in the blanks' in the personality type information I got from other methods. I was also thrilled to discover that knowing my magickal personality type helped me understand my behaviors and choices in my everyday life."
~ Gemma Kostadin, Phoenix, AZ

Define Your Goals:
Write, Light, and Be Bright

"If you have a goal, write it down. If you do not write it down, you do not have a goal – you have a wish."
~ Steve Maraboli

Time Required: Sixty Minutes per day for 40 days

Spoken words are more powerful than thoughts, just as written words are more manifestly "real" than spoken words. By writing down and prioritizing goals, you can use this simple magickal recipe to begin manifesting one goal at a time. Magickally, you will have better results if you focus on only one main goal at a time. All other goals must be subjugated to that single, most important goal.

Ingredients
- paper
- pen or pencil
- Sun Yellow candle (a bright yellow candle with no orange or red overtones)
- paper or wooden matches
- plate

Recipe Directions

1. Find a quiet spot where you will be undisturbed for at least an hour. Have your materials close by. In your chosen space, sit in the South facing North. Use a compass outdoors if you are unsure of the cardinal directions. Do not attempt to use your compass indoors as there are too many electromagnetic sources (televisions, computers, alarm systems, etc.) that can reduce the accuracy of a compass.

2. Take a moment to focus on your goals. Meditate on your goals until you are clear on the goal that is most important to you at this point in your life.

3. **Write**: Once you are clear on the single goal on which you choose to focus, start writing. Write down your chosen goal as precisely as possible while still allowing the Universe some flexibility in delivering your desire. For example, if your goal is to create a certain income goal for your business this year, write down a range of dollars (for instance, between $65,000.00 and $80,00.00), and a range of dates by which you want to achieve your goal. For instance, write down dates a few months before and after the one year mark.

   Magickally, you want to specify that the income be legally free and clear with no penalties and no death or loss of property to anyone. In addition, you may also wish to specify that the Universe not "bind" anyone in delivering your goal. Feel free to write your goal using bullet points so you can write all the specific parameters of your goal.

4. **Light**: Set your written goal aside for a moment. Be sure you are sitting in the South facing North. Put your plate in front of you, and then put the Sun Yellow candle in the middle of the plate. Place the

paper with your stated goal underneath the Sun Yellow candle and on top of the plate. Now light the candle with your match, and once the flame has settled into a tall and steady flame, cup your hands around the flame and in a voice of command say:

"Child of Wonder,
Child of Flame,
Nourish My Spirit
And Bring My Aim!"

5. You can repeat the phrase three to seven times to increase the force of this simple magickal spell. Leave the candle burning in a safe place for 30 to 60 minutes at a time. At the end of that time, blow out the candle. Blowing rather than snuffing the flame "sends" your request to the Universe. Repeat this ritual every single day for 40 days.

How to Use the Results of Your Recipe

While the Universe is working on manifesting your goal, your job (aside from doing the Sun Candle ritual described in the previous section) is to be bright. Keep an open mind and heart, look for possible signs that your goal is manifesting, and appreciate where you are. Appreciation of your current situation is one of the key magickal "tricks" to manifest your goals faster. You cannot move on to the next phase of your life journey until you have fully appreciated and accepted where you are today. In Earth School, of which we are all students, we cannot take the next step on our life journey until we have learned the lessons being offered in our current life situation.

Avoid being a Doubting Thomas. Find as much peace and joy as you can find. The Universe has a much easier time delivering to a bright and joyful recipient. After all, one of our "jobs" on this planet is to "sound a joyous note to Creator's ear" (according to the Hopi Indians). The more you can "be bright," as well as be consistent in doing the

Sun Yellow candle ritual, the more help you will get from the Universe.

You may notice results in the moments just after you complete the Sun Candle ritual, or you may notice events and occurrences related to your goal throughout your day. As you continue to do the Sun Candle ritual each day, you may sense new insights or guidance that appear in unexpected ways. For instance, you may be flipping through a magazine while you wait in line at the grocery store, and suddenly read a phrase that gives you inspiration, hope, or new perspective on your goal.

To add force to your "Write, Light, and Be Bright" ritual, actively seek at least one "thing" related to your goal. Your intention will act like a tractor beam to attract to you people, guides, angels, events, and opportunities that will aid you in manifesting your goals more quickly and easily. To add even more force, take the time daily to write down in a notebook every related beneficial force or sign or event helpful to your goal. Whenever you feel doubtful or unsure about your goal or about magick, flip through your notebook to bolster your spirits. Reading through this notebook will help you remain bright during the 40 days of this ritual.

Discover Your Magickal Type: What's Your Magickal Personality?

Time Required: Sixty Minutes

In magick, we work with four fundamental elements: Air, Fire, Water, and Earth. Understanding these magickal elements, how they manifest in our daily lives, and how they interact with each others helps any magickal practitioner. In our school, the Esoteric School of Shamanism and Magick, we have students prove the following hypothesis in the Basic Magic Course:

"If the four elements be understood in terms of their characteristics and correspondences, along with their interactions, a person can understand anything he or she wishes, in or about our Universe."

Each of the four magickal elements has its own characteristics associated with it. By knowing what these characteristics are in your personality, you'll be able to identify your strengths, how you view the world, and how you interact with the world and others. Having this knowledge gives you insight into ways to approach your goals, techniques to use, and even how to word them in a way that will be in sync with your energetic makeup. Most importantly, with regard to using magick to manifest your goals, knowing your elemental magickal personality allows you to predict the types of resistance your personality type may encounter.

Ingredients

- Four Element Personality Test (in the following section)
- Pen or Pencil to write answers and score

Recipe Directions

The elements that dominate your personality play a key role in determining how you deal with life issues, and, more importantly, how you help or hinder the manifestation of your goals.

Find out which elements dominate your personality type by filling out the form below. Look at the words on the left and right of each row, then mark the box (just one) in each row that most describes the way you actually are.

For instance, in the example below, if you're a somewhat feeling-oriented person you would check the box like this:

	Definitely	Somewhat	Somewhat	Definitely	
Feel	☐	☑	☐	☐	See

If you are a very visual person, and tend to "see" rather than "feel" your way through situations, you would check the box like this:

	Definitely	Somewhat	Somewhat	Definitely	
Feel	☐	☑	☐	☑	See

Take the Four Magickal Elements Personality Test

   Look at the pairs of words on either end of each row. First choose the word (on either the left or right side of the row) that most closely resembles your personality in everyday life. Next, decide whether the word <u>strongly</u> or only <u>somewhat</u> resembles your personality in everyday life. If the word strongly resembles your personality, choose the "Definitely" box that is next to your chosen word. Otherwise, choose the "Somewhat" box closest to your chosen word. Choose only one box per row, and mark one box on every row.

	Definitely	Somewhat	Definitely	Somewhat	
Ideas	❏	❏	❏	❏	Action
Go with the flow	❏	❏	❏	❏	Stability
Show	❏	❏	❏	❏	Tell
Desire	❏	❏	❏	❏	Compassion
Be	❏	❏	❏	❏	Do
Communicate	❏	❏	❏	❏	Create
Appreciate	❏	❏	❏	❏	Anticipate
Material	❏	❏	❏	❏	Spiritual
Adaptability	❏	❏	❏	❏	Security
Harmony	❏	❏	❏	❏	Excitement
Permanence	❏	❏	❏	❏	Change

Score Your Results

   Use the key below to score your four element personality test results. Each element below is represented by a single letter:

A = Air
F = Fire
W = Water
E = Earth

Each "Definitely" choice is given the score of 3 points, while each "Somewhat" choice is give a score of 1 point. Therefore, if you have A3 on a row, put 3 points in the Air Scoring Box below. Similarly, if you have W1, put 1 point in the Water Scoring Box.

	Definitely	Somewhat	Definitely	Somewhat	
Ideas	❑	❑	❑	❑	Action
	A3	A1	F1	F3	
Go with the flow	❑	❑	❑	❑	Stability
	W3	W1	E1	E3A3	
Show	❑	❑	❑	❑	Tell
	E3	E1	A1	A3	
Desire	❑	❑	❑	❑	Compassion
	F3	F1	W1	W3	
Be	❑	❑	❑	❑	Do
	E3	E1	F1	F3	
Communicate	❑	❑	❑	❑	Create
	A3	A1	F1	F3	
Appreciate	❑	❑	❑	❑	Anticipate
	W3	W1	A1	A3	
Material	❑	❑	❑	❑	Spiritual
	E3	E1	W1	W3	
Adaptability	❑	❑	❑	❑	Security
	A3	A1	E1	E3	
Harmony	❑	❑	❑	❑	Excitement
	W3	W1	F1	F3	
Permanence	❑	❑	❑	❑	Change
	E3	E1	F1	F3	

Once you have finished scoring your test, add the points in each element Scoring Box. Whichever elements have the highest score are the elements that dominate your personality.

Usually one or two elements score higher than the rest. For instance, if the Water score is the highest, that indicates that your personality is primarily Water. If, on the other hand, both Air and Fire are high, then your personality is an Air/Fire mix. Read the descriptions at the end of this test to find out more about your personality type.

Four Element Scoring Box

Air	Fire	Water	Earth

How to Use the Results of Your Recipe

Consider your goal in relation to these findings according to which elemental personality you discovered relates to you from taking the Test.

Air

If you are an Air personality you are a good communicator, planner, speaker and thinker. You are quick to come up with ideas, solutions and inspiration. You respond to ideas and visions, are great teachers and mediators who are able to easily absorb and translate large amounts of data. Personalities dominant in the Air element usually have excellent memories, but are also easily distracted by different ideas and are apt to change beliefs, opinions and ideas quite often. It is often a challenge for Air personalities to complete projects and tasks because of the distraction factor and because they prefer change and novelty to stability and practicality. Air personalities do well using their creativity and capitalizing on the ability to see the big picture.

Fire

If you are a Fire personality you are energetic, full of life, radiant, enthusiastic and achievement oriented. You are a mover and shaker, a person of action, creative, a natural leader, often courageous and value initiative and freedom. Fire personalities are constantly on the move, become excited easily and have lots of energy, power, will and desire. They often are people that do extreme sports and like life in the fast lane. Fire element personalities can also become easily frustrated when things are dragging or with lack of action on the part of others. This can cause them to become impatient, irritable and to act spontaneously without thinking first. Fire people will do well to find life roles that allow them express their passion, creativity, and enthusiasm. They will struggle with learning to think before acting, but will do well to be aware of this and work on it.

Water

If you are a Water personality you are an empathetic and compassionate person. Other people often turn to you for comfort, love and assurance. You may be involved in causes that take care of others and the planet. Empaths, psychics and healers are often Water personalities. Integrity, compassion, harmony, creating balance and interacting with integrity can all be Water personality values. These type of people are appreciative of beauty and gifts in life. Since they do have a characteristic of empathy so ingrained in their personalities, Water people may find themselves getting over involved in other people's emotions and problems and often taking on their negative energies. They often become over invested in others and take on a caretaking role mistaking that for love. People of this personality type must guard against trying to save or fix everyone and everything and realize that they can better serve through modeling appreciation, gratitude and joy. Water personalities will do well in roles in which they are empowered to use their intuitive and empathetic gifts. They need to have interaction with other people, plants, animals or spirit beings to feed their souls. They will also thrive in situations that allow them to spread their appreciation of beauty and joy, and in situations that allow the Water person to express who they are and stay true to their values.

Earth

If you are an Earth personality you are a practical and pragmatic person. You are a down to earth person with much strength, endurance, patience and persistence. Structure, boundaries, loyalty and permanence are things that you value. Earth personalities are often good at commerce and build strong foundations in their relationships and lives. Earth people are great at manifesting their goals, are often builders, and do well in situations that they can add structure to. They want to know how things work and often fool around with improving everything. They are solid people that others drift to in uncertain times or see as an anchor or a "rock" and very often are very serene people. The challenge for Earth people is not getting stuck in a rut. Their desire for stability can often lead to stubbornness and inflexibility. They err on the side of caution, make decisions slowly and usually avoid taking risks. Another challenge for Earth people is their tendency to get bogged down with too many material possessions, especially large ones. Earth personalities will do well in roles and situations that allow them to exercise their practicality and love of structure. Earth people should avoid situations with lots of quick change and too much risk taking. A good challenge for an Earth person however is in learning to take some risks periodically.

The Four Magickal Elements

Each of the four elements has its own characteristics associated with it. By knowing what these characteristics are, you'll be able to identify what your strengths are, how you view the world and how you interact with the world and others. This knowledge can help you find the career you are best suited for, know the type of people you are most compatible with when looking for friends or a mate, and give you an understanding of the best way for you to approach situations in your life. It also makes you aware of your challenges so you will be prepared to encounter resistance or difficult situations with a plan for dealing with them already in place. Once you know which of the magical four elements is dominant in your personality by taking the magical personality test, you not only get a better understanding of yourself, but also start looking at others and any situation you encounter in relation to the elements and how best for you to interact with them.

Goal Magick Recipes

Main Course: Define the Details of the Goal, and Stay the Course

Success is in the Details: Write Directors and Limiters for Your Goal

Boost the Sun Candle: Add Directors and Limiters, a Keyed Plate, and a Magnet to the Ritual

Reduce Resistance: Let the Walking Meditation Highlight Obstacles

"Amazement is the best word to describe the benefits from writing the details for my goal. These details really made me think about what I wanted and didn't want in the manifestation of my goal. Then adding the extra boost to the Sun Candle ritual brought my goal to me even faster. But perhaps the best ritual for me was the Walking Litany... I never knew how much I got in my own way. Thumbs up all the way around!"
~ Bobbi Janiston, Macon, GA

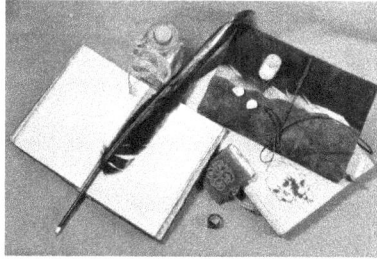

Success is in the Details:
Write Directors and Limiters
for Your Goal

"To create something exceptional, your mindset must be relentlessly focused on the smallest detail."
~ Giorgio Armani

Time Required: Sixty Minutes

When using goal magick, it is very important to be precise. Magic is a precision science. The Universe can always deliver what we ask for, but sometimes it doesn't seem that way because we are not specific enough in our request. In other words, our requests for the Universe to manifest our goals lacks the necessary details.

Let's say for example that you want extra money. You are ready to receive this money, and you have asked the Universe to deliver. As you are walking down the street, you look down and find a penny. There you go, the Universe delivered just what you asked for... extra money. What you didn't do was specify how much money or when you needed it by or that you don't want anyone else to come to harm in order for you to attain it. This is where Directors and Limiters can help us become more precise in letting the Universe know exactly what we want.

Directors

The list of Directors tells the Universe in detail everything you want the Universe to manifest with regards to your goal. In this list include specifically exactly what you want: how much money, date you want it by, etc. When writing Directors, it is often better to define ranges rather than absolutes to give the Universe room to work. For example, it is often better to write "delivered in six to ten weeks" rather than saying "must come at 4:00 pm on October 2, 20xx." Also, do NOT specify HOW your goal will manifest. It is the Universe's job to determine the delivery system.

Limiters

Limiters are a list of what you choose to exclude from your goal manifestation. It is a way to safeguard yourself and others. Remember that according to Rules of the Road (found in the section "A Few Rules and Tips About Kitchen Table Magick") that causing harm to others will provide a backlash to you, whether in this lifetime or a future one, and whether you did it with intention or not. Use your Limiters to define details, such as wanting your money to come to you without causing the death or loss of property to any of your family or friends. You might also want to specify in the Limiters that there not be any negative financial surprises to pop up around the money, for example some type of large tax or investment of capital on your part. As always in magick, think it through completely, and then build in your safeguards.

Ingredients

- paper
- pen or pencil
- some uninterrupted quiet time

Recipe Directions

1. When you sit down to write your Directors and Limiters, take your time to really think through what you are asking for before you write your Directors and Limiters. Think of ways that what you are asking for could come to you and write Limiters around those scenarios that you do not want it to happen through. Anything you leave to chance will follow the path of least resistance and may achieve your goal, but in a way that you didn't want. You also need to be reasonable with your goal and the time frame to accomplish it. For instance, it is not reasonable to ask that a million dollars appears tomorrow.

2. Once you have taken some time to meditate on your goal, begin by writing your Directors, To give you an example of what your lists may look like, here are some Directors for the goal of attracting a mate:

   Directors:
   A man (or woman) who:
   - is between the ages of 30 and 40
   - lives within 100 miles of you
   - has a steady job and earns between $x and $y
   - shares similar interests as you (you might want to get specific here)
   - has a certain kind of personality
   - has any other desired characteristics

3. After reviewing your Directors and editing them until you feel they are complete (though these can be edited any time), it's time to turn your attention to writing your Limiters. When writing Limiters, consider the worst-case scenarios and limit them with your Limiters. For instance, you don't want your spell to cause anyone to die. You probably don't want the spell to result in loss of property or income for yourself or your family or your dog, etc. You don't

want your spell to cause you do to anything illegal. Be sure to write your Limiters to include these scenarios.

One magical practitioner wrote a "get a job" spell and forgot to exclude jobs that required illegal activity. The spell brought her the most fantastic job with great pay and fabulous working hours. The only catch was that she ended up working for the mob.

To give you a feeling of how a set of Limiters may look, here are some Limiters for the goal of attracting a mate:

Limiters
A man (or woman) who:
- does not have any pre-existing health issues
- does not have any children from previous marriages
- plus any other limiters you do not want to bring into a new relationship

4. Once you have written your list of Directors and Limiters, put your list away for the day.

5. The following day, pull out your list and review it with fresh eyes. Make any edits to your lists, and then print out a clean copy of the Directors and Limiters. Have these lists ready for the magickal ritual defined in the next recipe.

How to Use the Results of Your Recipe
Once you have a solid and specific list of Directors and Limiters, you may want to write verses to accompany your Directors and Limiters. Verses are lyrical or poetic versions of your Directors and Limiters, and can be used in conjunction with your Directors and Limiters to strengthen your spell. For instance, in the next ritual, you will add your

Directors and Limiters to the ritual. As you light the Sun Candle each day, keep the Directors and Limiters under the candle while you read your verses aloud in a voice of command. Taking the time to write verses and read them daily (often for 40 days at a time) sends a strong signal to the Universe. While verses are not strictly necessary, the lyrical vocalization of your spell on a daily basis roots your spell deeper in your psyche, and attracts that which you desire into your life more quickly.

Here is a sample of verses so you can get a "feel" for how they can flow:

House Finding Spell
To find a house quickly, I do this spell
Build the energy, spread the work, my allies tell.
As candle burns so start this magical force
Fulfill directors and limiters, go to the source
Where help is ready to see this project through
And all our needs be met, our state wishes do.

A house for rent, spacious and well-kept, clean
In April be available, by Betsy and David can be seen.
Four bedrooms at least and bathrooms three or two
Spacious yard, safe for Tether, and quiet with a view.

Large kitchen, family rooms, a sacred place to be
For Tether, our friends, and each of us three.

A place for ritual, wood-working, and for my work
Where who we are and what we do causes no one irk.
For two years minimum, exceed not 1200 monthly to pay
Agreeable landlord or lady, happy for us to stay.

Help Betsy and David to carry on their search
So as of May first we have a new place to perch.

Good luck, take your time, think it through, do it right, and have fun! Magick done well is both practical and delightful!

Boost the Sun Candle:
Add Directors and Limiters, a Keyed Plate, and a Magnet to the Ritual

"Set a goal and do something about it every day."
~ Mary Kay

Time Required: Sixty Minutes per day for 40 days

If you have been doing the Sun Candle Ritual from an earlier section of this book then you have probably felt or seen some results. Some of our students report seeing "small signs" that their goals are manifesting on a daily basis. For instance, one student received a "sign" related to her goal daily, whether it was a word or phrase related to her goal that popped up in an article she was reading, or seeing a small step forward toward her goal, such as being assigned as an assistant project manager at work.

Now you can boost the power of the Sun Candle Ritual by adding your Directors and Limiters, plus a magnet and a magickally keyed plate. Your Directors and Limiters will closely define the scope of your goal, which gives the Universe greater focus and efficiency in defining your goals. The magnet will help you continue to attract your goal into your life even when the Sun Candle is not burning.

Ingredients

- your Directors and Limiters
- Sun Yellow candle (a bright yellow candle with no orange or red overtones)
- paper or wooden matches
- plate
- a source of grass green color you can easily see while you perform the Recipe Directions
- large magnet (about 1" long x .5" wide x .25" thick), which can be found at most hardware stores

Recipe Directions

Using the Sun Candle Ritual, with or without a magnet, is often referred to in magickal circles as a "come along." These rituals act as a "come along" in that they bring or attract your goals to you, much as the fishing line on a fishing pole reels in a fish. Keying your plate magickally, which personalizes the plate to your personal energies (and thus your goal), adds further "pull" to your "come along." In other words, adding these ingredients to the ordinary Sun Candle Ritual will only attract your goal with greater force. To perform all the directions in the following section, gather your materials, and sit in the South facing North.

1. Magickally key your plate so that you can add even greater attractive power to your Sun Candle Ritual. Once your plate is keyed it becomes a magickal Plate or Pantacle.

   - Place your hands on either side of your plate
   - Grip the plate with your thumbs on the top surface of the plate and the rest of your fingers supporting the underside of the plate.
   - Look at a grass green energy color source, and begin flowing that energy from your dominant hand (hand with which you normally point) through the plate into your other hand

- Keep the energy flowing up your arm, across your shoulders, down the arm of your dominant hand and out your output hand again
- Circulate grass green energy for about three minutes, then pull that energy back into your body.
- You will know the plate is keyed when it feels slightly tingly, heavy, warm or loaded or definitely different than before you keyed it in some way. You now have a magickally keyed Plate or Pantacle.

2. Now place your Plate in front of you. Put your Directors and Limiters on your Plate, and put the Sun Candle on top of the Directors and Limiters. Follow the same procedures as previously given for the Sun Candle Ritual, leaving the Sun Candle burning for 30 to 60 minutes.

3. Once you have blown out the Sun Candle, replace the candle with your magnet. The magnet will continue to attract your goal, as defined in detail by your Directors and Limiters, even though the Sun Candle is not lit.

How to Use the Results of Your Recipe

Once you begin using the "boosted" Sun Candle Ritual, begin looking for more signs from magickal powers and beings that your goal is becoming manifest. Keep your ears open for random phrases related to your goals. These phrases will often emerge from conversations between strangers. Look for meaningful words as you leaf through magazines while waiting in the checkout line. Or look for more subtle hints. Some people feel more energized while working toward their goals, while others become inspired by new ideas and directions related toward their goals.

Reduce Resistance: Let the Walking Meditation Highlight Obstacles

"If you have time to breathe you have time to meditate. You breathe when you walk. You breathe when you stand. You breathe when you lie down."
~ Ajahn Amaro

Time Required: Fifteen Minutes

In a previous section you discovered your magickal personality type. As with any aspects of our personalities, there are both benefits and downsides. Some parts of your magickal personality type will help you manifest your goal, while other parts of your personality type will create resistance to your goal.

If you have difficulty being still long enough to do sitting meditations, the Walking Meditation may be the perfect form of meditation for you. Meditation, or communication with higher powers and beings, is important. Higher powers and beings can easily point out which parts of your magickal personality type are creating resistance, as well as the steps you can take to reduce or eliminate that resistance.

As you may have read in our other materials, certain higher powers and beings are just waiting to be asked for help and information. One just has to ask, give thanks in advance, and wait for the information to flow into your life. The Walking Meditation is the perfect way to request help from the appropriate powers and beings, and receive feedback... all in a simple magickal walk.

Ingredients

- A space of about 15 minutes when you can walk alone, without interruption from other people, cell phones, or other digital media.
- Preferably a quiet nature path, but a good magickal practitioner can gain the benefits of the Walking Litany even on the busiest of streets

Recipe Directions

1. Choose an amount of time you will walk or a distance you will walk. Should be at least the distance of two city blocks. Be prepared to walk at least two city blocks or the equivalent distance on a nature path.

2. As you begin walking, talk to your totems, guides, angels, the Universe or any higher beings about whatever is on your mind, what you need, or what you want as related to your goal. Specifically, you may wish to inquire as to how your magickal personality type may be causing resistance in the manifestation of your goal. You will do the talking for the first half of the walk. Feel free to speak aloud or ask your questions silently in your mind.

3. After you have requested all the help and knowledge you wish to have from Higher Powers and Beings, give your thanks beforehand. Angels, totems, and all

kinds of higher beings thrive on gratitude as their favorite form of energy exchange.

4. Halfway through the walk, stop talking and begin listening and watching for signs of feedback from the powers you have been talking to.

How to Use the Results of Your Recipe

As you walk, feel your feelings, be aware of body sensations, listen to the sounds around you, smell the smells around you and really see the sights around you. Absorb all these things totally. Listen not just with your ears, but with your whole being.

Do not be discouraged if, at first, you don't immediately receive full answers to all of your questions and requests. Be patient. Keep asking, and keep listening, not just during your Meditation, but throughout your day. If you receive answers that are not clear, ask for clarification during your next Walking Meditation. Higher Powers and Beings are always happy to clarify. Just ask them to provide information in ways that *you* can clearly understand. And remember to always give thanks in advance. Higher Powers and Beings need nothing more.

If you can persist with the Walking Meditation for a number of days, or whenever you need answers, prepare to be amazed. You will receive all the answers you need about how to reduce the resistance your magickal personality type might create. With reduced resistance, your goal will manifest in your life faster than you can ever imagine.

Goal Magick Recipes

Desserts: Inspiration is the Cherry on Top!

Choose Your Price: It's Not What You Think

Plan for the "Inconvenience Factor'

"When I read that I had to 'pay a price' to achieve my goal I wanted to stop reading. I am so glad that I kept reading because I found that the price I paid really just meant letting go of something no longer useful in my life. Releasing old 'stuff' from my life also allowed me to make a plan to deal with personality resistance."
~ Joan Augustine, Baltimore, MD

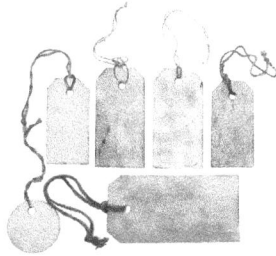

Choose Your Price:
It's Not What You Think

"You create your own universe as you go along."
~ Winston Churchill

Time Required: Thirty Minutes

Since we live on a planet where virtually nothing is free, our minds tell us that the Universe must demand a price for the gifts and benefits it bestows on us. When it comes to getting something we want, our minds follow the thought process of:

a) I would love to have X (something I don't have and feel is beyond my current reach)
b) I can't afford X
c) Darn! Forget about X.

The truth is that the Universe doesn't work that way and does not demand a price from us. The Universe and its angelic and other spiritual helpers operates on a larger and grander scale than we do on Earth. What we consider a miracle is just an everyday occurrence to them. It doesn't consider demanding a price from us anymore than we would demand a price for holding a door open for someone with hands full of packages. To get around this belief that you must provide "payment," follow this recipe. With this recipe you will choose your own price to pay to reach your goal so that you can feel like you have "paid into" your goal. For most people this provides a sense of relief, which makes space in life to allow the goal to manifest.

Ingredients
- A quiet period of time when you can focus on choosing the "price" you will pay for your goal
- Pen and paper to jot down ideas

Recipe Directions
When choosing your price you choose to pay for your goal, there are certain issues to take into consideration. The price you choose to pay the Universe is most likely not what you expect. Read the following sections before choosing your price. Then jot down ideas of possible "price" options you might choose.

1. **Money**: The price doesn't have to be money. The Universe doesn't really have any use for money. That is a human concept. Your price could involve money if you wanted to donate to charity or something along that line, but it does not HAVE to be money and may be best if it is not. Just the mere mention of money often makes people feel anxious, stressed, angry, regretful or a slew of other negative type emotions. For that reason it is probably best just to keep money out of it.

2. **Sacrifice:** You could pick a price that includes sacrificing something you don't really need. That could mean getting rid of possessions, which could create more sacred space in your life. Another option would be to get rid of emotional states like anger, impatience, doubt, fear or any type of negative

energies that interfere with your life. The same could apply to negative thoughts that you continually have. Sacrificing a thought means replacing it with something else. Instead of allowing your mind to repeat negative thoughts over and over, stop and change to a positive thought. Sometimes this process means you have to just start with a simple "I am willing to be willing to think a more positive thought" instead of jumping right to the positive thought itself. The same process works for dealing with negative emotions.

3. **Mutual Benefit:** You could pick a price that will have benefit for you and for another person by being of service to them. This "pay it forward" philosophy can have a lot of great benefits. When you "pay it forward," you satisfy your mind by letting it believe you have made your payment and are now ready and deserving to receive your gift from the Universe. Acts of service could be those where you do something for someone and you don't tell anyone what you have done or that you have done anything at all. It doesn't have to be a big thing that you do however. It could be that you send blessings to someone you pass on the street that looks like they are having a bad day. Maybe you just hold the door for someone else or give them a flower from your garden. You could simply allow a negative comment from another person without arguing with the speaker. Or just take off work early to spend some extra time with your family.

4. **Good for You:** For the most part, when we think of paying a price, we think that we will possess less of something we value. For instance, when we pay for an item at a store, we reduce our bank accounts by a certain amount. Therefore paying a price means that we reduce the amount of something we value: money. Instead, you can choose a price that actually

increases something of value in your life. For instance, you could choose to work out three times a week as your price. Why does this qualify as a price? Because you have to pay into the discipline required to work out on a regular basis. At the same time, this "price" increases rather than reduces something you value: physical fitness and a better body.

How to Use the Results of Your Recipe

Once you have written some ideas of possible "price" options, you can choose your price right away, or you can allow the list to sit for a few days. Some students find the "Three Day Option" works the best. With this option, you put the list away, and avoid thinking about the whole topic of "choosing your price" for three days. Any time you find yourself thinking about the topic, simply think about any other topic. Then on the third day, pull out your list and choose your price.

The price you select does not matter. Whether the price is large or small does not matter because, after all, it is your choice. Choose a price that is reasonable and will satisfy your mental thought that "nothing is free." Remember it's all for you because the Universe really doesn't demand the price. No matter what price you pick, if that price helps put you in a better space to receive from the Universe, then the price is well worth it.

Plan for the "Inconvenience Factor"

"Change is not made without inconvenience, even from worse to better."
~ Richard Hooker

Time Required: Thirty Minutes

The majority of people who want to practice magick don't consider the factors involved in walking a magickal path. Most people say, "I want magic in my life!" and stop there. But that kind of mentality doesn't work.

Magic is a precision science, which means that if you want to have magic in your life, you need to define precisely what kind of magic you want in your life ... and how much of it. Why do you need to answer these questions before inviting magic into your life? Multiple reasons ...

1. Magic always works but sometimes its effect is difficult to see. If you don't define exactly what you want, chances are that magic will manifest in your life and you won't even know it! This is the very reason you created detailed Directors and Limiters for your Sun Candle Ritual.

2. Magic, improperly handled, can wreak havoc in your life! One woman did a spell to pay off her credit card

debt, but never specified PRECISELY how the spell should work. Her husband died and his life insurance policy was just enough to pay off the credit card debt. The magic worked ... just not in the way the practitioner wanted. This is another reason for you to create Directors and Limiters.

3. You need to prepare yourself and your life for magic. You need to make space in your life for magic in terms of the kind of practice you are willing to do, the amount of time you are willing to spend learning and using what you learn, and the amount of inconvenience you are willing to accept into your life. Hence, you took steps to reduce the resistance caused by your magickal personality type, and also chose a magickal "price" to free up your mind from the idea that "nothing is free."

<u>What is the "Inconvenience Factor"?</u>

One of the things students of magick do not expect is the amount of inconvenience that shows up in their lives as a result. But some amount of inconvenience is simply a part of walking the magickal path. Magic is, well, quite magical, but taking on a magical practice often means a lot of inconvenience at the life level. It has been our observation, through the teaching of many classes, that students of magic come up against this inconvenience factor from the beginning of our studies and onward. At some time in your training it is inevitable that taking the time and making the effort to learn and use magical techniques will become highly inconvenient.

For some people, the inconvenience factor manifests in making uncomfortable "choices" about keeping up the study of magick because of phone or car problems, work related demands, family affairs, or any of a myriad of drastic life events. This may require you to make small, even sometimes radical changes in your lives. Be aware of the inconvenience factor before you invite magick into your life, and as you begin and continue with your practice. We

tell you this not to discourage you... only to give fair
warning!

Ingredients
- Pen and paper
- Sun Candle
- Some quiet time for brainstorming

Recipe Directions
1. Gather your materials and sit in the East facing
   East. The East is the direction of ideas and
   knowledge (and also the direction associated with
   the magickal element Air, the element of
   communication, ideas, and enlightenment).

2. Follow the directions offered in earlier rituals to
   light and "charge" your Sun Candle using the
   verse given in an earlier recipe (starts with "Child
   of Wonder..."). The Sun Candle will inspire new
   ideas as you brainstorm.

3. Spend a few minutes in quiet meditation. Focus
   on the factors in your life that have seemed most
   inconvenient or caused you to feel the most
   helpless or hopeless.

4. Feeling the energy from your Sun Candle and
   from the direction East, jot down the types of
   events and incidences that are most likely to
   cause you to feel the "inconvenience factor."
   These events could include car trouble, computer
   break downs, family drama, money shortages,
   difficult bosses, or even severe weather.

5. Keep your list of possible inconvenient factors
   handy during the days to come as you may think
   of more items to add to the list.

How to Use the Results of Your Recipe

Once you have a fairly complete list of "inconvenient" items, keep the list with you. When something unexpected and "inconvenient" shows up in your life, consult your list. Ask yourself whether this issue is simply a manifestation of the "inconvenience factor." If so, then know that by being resourceful you can find many ways to get past this inconvenient event.

Most issues that fall under the "inconvenience factor" are solved far more easily and with far less expense than issues that are just a normal part of life. For instance, if your car breaks down because of the "inconvenience factor," the cost to fix it is most likely less than if your car breaks down as a normal part of the chaos of life.

The way to distinguish normal life events from events that are part of the "inconvenience factor" is to consider whether the event is a chain of events or a recurring event that is keeping you specifically from working on your goal magick. If so, then the events are part of the magickal inconvenience that is simply a part of the magickal path. If the unexpected event is NOT keeping you from your magickal practices, then chances are that the event is simply a random life event.

As a magickal practitioner, one way to use magick most effectively to manifest your goals in your life is to deal with issues related to the "inconvenience factor" as quickly and efficiently as possible. Also, approach the issue with a strong sense of knowing that the problem can be solved far more easily than appearances may suggest.

The good news is that in choosing your "price" to pay for your goal magick (from an earlier section), you are less likely to experience the "inconvenience" factor than magickal practitioners who do not choose a price to pay. So face those inconvenient events with a smile and a sure hand, and you will have very little problem handling these issues!

More Magickal Resources

Kindle or Paperback on Amazon:
Witchcraft Spell Book Series:
Learn How to Do Witchcraft Rituals and Spells with Your Bare Hands (Witchcraft Spell Books, Book 1)

Learn How to Do Witchcraft Rituals and Spells with Household Ingredients (Witchcraft Spell Books, Book 2)

Learn How to Do Witchcraft Rituals and Spells with Magical Tools (Witchcraft Spell Books, Book 3)

Witchcraft Spell Book: The Complete Guide of Witchcraft Rituals & Spells for Beginners (compilation of Books 1, 2 & 3)

Kitchen Table Magick Series

Ebooks and Online Courses at www.shamanschool.com
Wand: Air Tool
Athame: Fire Tool
Chalice: Water Tool
Plate: Earth Tool
Magical Tool: Firebowl
Psychic Development
Energy Healing For Self and Others
How to Do Voodoo
Daily Rituals to Attract What You Want in Life

Find a complete list of magickal resources on G. Alan Joel's Author Page. These resources are constantly updated so check back often!

Free Gift Offer

To thank you for purchasing this book, I'd like to give you a

100% FREE GIFT

Learn more about your free gift.

Click Here to Access Your Free Gift

Like What You Read? Spread the Magick and Leave a Review

Find a complete list of magickal resources on G. Alan Joel's Author Page. These resources are constantly updated so check back often!

About G. Alan Joel

Magick means many things to different people. The form of magick taught by G. Alan Joel for more than 30 years is steeped in tribal traditions from around the world, from both modern tribal cultures and those from the past, which have been mostly passed on through oral dialog.

At the very heart of the magick that Mr. Joel teaches is the use of Universal Laws for the benefit of self, others, and even the planet. These magickal traditions can take on many forms, including simple rituals for daily use, specific spells for particular life situations, the use of simulacra (often better known as voodoo), weather working, water witching, the use of the elemental tools (Firebowl, Wand, Athame, Chalice, and Plate), magickal self-defense rituals, and more. Also included are the use of the Tarot for divination and spellwork, divination rituals of all kinds, Spirit-to-Spirit communication, exercises for psychic development, and abundant healing techniques.

Through his 30 plus years of studying, teaching, and honing his magickal practice, G. Alan Joel has helped thousands of people successfully integrate the magickal, and seemingly miraculous, into their daily lives. In fact, one of the greatest gifts Mr. Joel has offered through his teachings is the ability for his students to always find a magickal solution for life situations that often seem impossible to solve. With magick, anything is possible in the mundane world. All that is required of the practitioner is an open mind, the desire to learn, and a willingness to pay some time and effort into his or her magickal practice. One of Mr. Joel's favorite quotes is:

"What you pay into your practice pays you back!"

While many magickal traditions have fiercely guarded their secrets from the public, Mr. Joel feels that "Magick is the birthright of every planetary citizen." As such he strives to offer magickal teachings that are easily learned and inexpensive (no excessive fees to join exclusive magickal groups or ascend up the levels of learning). He also offers techniques that are usable and effective for all who are sincere in their desire to practice magick. In essence, Mr. Joel's methods teach a form of "Every Man's (and Woman's) Magick." All are welcome. His teachings are simple. yet effective, and he also offers online classes in which he helps students troubleshoot their magickal issues in an interactive setting.

Find out more about Mr. Joel's teachings here and on his website (www.shamanschool.com) where magickal offerings are updated on a regular basis.

Mr. Joel augments this magickal knowledge and teaching with 30 years of practice as Doctor of Chinese Medicine, including a deep understanding of herbology and acupuncture. His understanding of the healing arts deepens the magickal knowledge he teaches, as magickal healing is a major aspect of his teachings. Mr. Joel believes that while there is clearly a time and place for Western Medicine, magickal and Eastern healing techniques can be harmoniously blended in to offer people many choices for healing all types of health conditions.

About the Esoteric School of Shamanism and Magic

The Esoteric School of Shamanism and Magic was started from a desire for all people from all over the globe to be able to attend a real, if virtual, school dedicated to magick and shamanism. The aim of the Esoteric School of Shamanism and Magic is to help people create permanent, positive change in their lives through the study of esoteric magickal and shamanic knowledge. It doesn't matter what your esoteric background is, whether you started out with witchcraft, religious studies, spirituality or candle magick, we welcome you. We believe that the Truth is the same, no matter which form you practice. We delight in all manner of shamanic schools and traditions, magickal techniques and esoteric ritual. You can visit us at www.shamanschool.com, our blog at http://shamanmagic.blogspot.com/, or on Facebook at www.facebook.com/EsotericSchool.

www.ingramcontent.com/pod-product-compliance
Lightning Source LLC
Chambersburg PA
CBHW070554030426
42337CB00016B/2494